SPECIAL EDUCATIONAL NEEDS

POLICY OPTIONS STEERING GROUP

POLICY PAPER 2:

INCLUSION OR EXCLUSION:

Future Policy for Emotional and Behavioural Difficulties

Published in 1997

ISBN 0 906730 95 3

Published by NASEN Enterprises Ltd.
NASEN Enterprises is a company limited by guarantee, registered in England and Wales. Company No. 2637438.

Further copies of this book and details of NASEN's many other publications may be obtained from the Publications Department at its registered office: NASEN House, 4/5, Amber Business Village, Amber Close, Amington, Tamworth, Staffs. B77 4RP.
Tel: 01827 311500; Fax: 01827 313005

Cover design by Graphic Images.
Typeset in Times by J. C. Typesetting and printed in the United Kingdom by Stowes, Stoke-on-Trent.

Contents

This paper was edited by Brahm Norwich

3

Introduction – This Policy Paper

This paper is a record of a recent invited Policy Seminar held at the Institute of Education looking at New Dimensions of Educational Policy and Practice for Children and Young People with Emotional and Behavioural Difficulties. Three papers were presented, one by a Child Psychiatrist, Dr Greg Richardson, a second by an officer from a teachers' association, John Bangs from the National Union of Teachers, and a third by a Principal Educational Psychologist, Peter Gray, though his paper was presented by Tony Dessent, a Director of Education. Seminar participants included teachers and headteachers from mainstream and special schools, educational psychologists, Directors of Education, LEA officers, heads of support services, representatives from OFSTED, DfEE, representatives from relevant voluntary associations, such as MIND, NASEN, academics and educational researchers. The paper also includes summaries of small group and plenary discussions following the papers.

SEN Policy Options Steering Group
Background

This policy paper is the second one in the new second round of seminars and conferences to be organised by the SEN POLICY OPTIONS STEERING GROUP. This group organised the successful ESRC - Cadbury Trust series on policy analysis and policy options for special educational needs in the 1990s. (See the list of these policy papers published by NASEN at the end of this section.) It has representatives from LEA administrators, headteachers, voluntary organisations, professional associations, universities and research. Given the success of the first round of policy seminars and papers, a further round of seminars and conferences in this field has been undertaken. These events are intended to consider current and future policy issues in the field in a pro-active way. They are planned to interest all those concerned with policy matters in special educational needs.

Aims and objectives of the Policy Options Group

1. To identify current and likely future policy problems and the options for solutions in special education provision through to the year 2000;

2. to organise conferences and seminars for policy-makers, professionals, parents, voluntary associations and researchers in the field and publish the proceedings for wider dissemination;

3. To enhance the two-way relationship between policy and service issues and research agendas.

Current Steering Group membership
Mr Clive Danks, Headteacher; Professor Ron Davie, National Association of Special Educational Needs (NASEN) representative; Mr Tony Dessent, Director of Education, Luton LEA; Dr Seamus Hegarty, Director of the National Foundation for Educational Research; Professor Geoff Lindsay, Warwick University; Dr Ingrid Lunt, Senior Lecturer, Institute of Education, London University; Mr Vincent McDonnell, Principal Education Officer, Staffordshire LEA; Mr Chris Marshall, OFSTED; Professor Peter Mittler, Manchester University; Professor Brahm Norwich, Institute of Education, London University; Mrs Margaret Peter; Mrs Philippa Russell, Director of Council for Disabled Children; Professor Klaus Wedell, Institute of Education, London University.

Current programme
Problems and solutions in developing special educational provision
The current programme aims to organise four full or half day events on special education policy and provision over the two years 1995/96 - 1996/97 which are relevant to the context of considerable changes in the education system.

The first event in March 1996 was a seminar on local government reorganisation: issues about independence and inter-dependence arising from the new unitary and future county authorities. This policy paper has been published. See details below.

The next seminar, about developing policy to meet the challenges associated with emotional and behavioural difficulties, was held in February 1997. This paper records the outcomes of this seminar.

If you have any ideas about possible topics or would like to know more about the events, please do contact a member of the group or Brahm Norwich at 25 Woburn Square, London WC1H 0AA.

Policy Options Papers from first seminar series published and available from NASEN.

1. **Bucking the market**
   Peter Housden, Chief Education Officer, Nottinghamshire LEA.

2. **Towards effective schools for all**
   Mel Ainscow, Cambridge University Institute of Education.

3. **Teacher education for special educational needs**
   Professor Peter Mittler, Manchester University.

4. **Resourcing for SEN**
   Jennifer Evans and Ingrid Lunt, Institute of Education, London University.

5. **Special schools and their alternatives**
   Max Hunt, Director of Education, Stockport LEA.

6. **Meeting SEN: options for partnership between health, education and social services**
   Tony Dessent, Senior Assistant Director, Nottinghamshire LEA.

7. **SEN in the 1990s: users' perspectives**
   Micheline Mason, Robina Mallet, Colin Low and Philippa Russell.

Policy Options Papers from second seminar series published and available from NASEN.

1. **Independence or Interdependence? Responsibilities for SEN in the Unitary and County Authorities.**
   Roy Atkinson, Michael Peters, Derek Jones, Simon Gardner and Philippa Russell.

Educational Policy and Practice for Children and Young People with EBD

JOHN BANGS, Assistant Secretary, Education and Equal
Opportunities, National Union of Teachers. (In a personal capacity.)

Introduction

I welcome the opportunity to contribute to the Policy Seminar. The position I want to start from is based on the following framework.

In October 1996 Doug McAvoy, the NUT's General Secretary, wrote an article for *The Times Educational Supplement* which I think it is worth paraphrasing as the basis for what I want to say in my presentation. At certain points I have brought the article up to date.

Teachers currently experience a poisonous combination of circumstances. Their professionalism is challenged, they are told by the Government that the performance of many teachers does not meet Government-imposed targets, and in schools the job of teaching has become increasingly more demanding. Increased pressure on teachers comes from a variety of quarters. The Government's imposed accountability mechanisms have impinged heavily on the act of teaching itself. Class sizes have risen and the slow drip of constant, ill-informed criticism from the press and the Government has contributed to undermining morale. Added to these circumstances is another development. Many teachers will tell you that the behaviour of a significant (and growing) minority of pupils is getting worse.

The Government (this and all subsequent references refer to the ex-Conservative Government) has introduced legislation on pupil discipline and behaviour. There are new elements to that legislation, particularly the proposal that LEAs be required to produce behaviour plans and new clauses on pupil exclusions and on the restraint of pupils. The effect of this proposal has yet to be determined. However it is worth exploring teachers' perceptions.

When a child hurls a chair across a classroom or persistently abuses a teacher, despite being subjected to every behaviour strategy known to education, the teacher involved needs to know two things: how to stop the situation now and how to prevent it occurring again. At that moment, explanations of the cause are not at the forefront of the minds of the teacher and the other pupils. For the majority of pupils such a child presents exactly the same problem. Children and young people deeply resent their learning being interrupted by other pupils.

If teachers do not receive backing for their professional judgement from their employers or governing bodies, it is for their professional organisation

8

to step in and give support. In this situation, the NUT acts unequivocally and effectively to support teachers. We will sanction industrial action up to and including strike action where pupils who have been excluded are returned to schools by governing bodies, appeals panels or local education authorities against the professional judgement of the headteacher and the teaching staff. We have been giving this support without hesitation and with success for a very long time; indeed as long as such incidents have occurred.

We do not seek publicity for these cases. Media attention can mean that others can identify the pupil concerned publicly. In addition, quiet negotiation can lead to the parents or the pupil accepting alternative schooling without dispute.

However, finding solutions to individual cases is not the same as finding solutions to the underlying problem. Some of the changes to legislation will help teachers, but a more fundamental change is needed. The increase in the numbers of pupils with behavioural problems is matched almost precisely by the rate of Government-inspired decline of support to teachers with such pupils.

School counsellors have all but disappeared from our secondary schools. Teachers have found themselves compelled to switch from meeting pastoral and special needs to complying with the demands of an overloaded National Curriculum. All this without support. Since 1988 the Government has, in effect, sanctioned the removal of many support services by cutting centrally held LEA resources, an action which will be compounded by current Government proposals for LMS if they come to pass.

That statement encapsulates the NUT's thinking. What I want to do is to explore a number of issues arising from that position and to explore them under a number of headings.

Reasonable Expectations

I will not explore the key characteristics of school improvement. They will be familiar to you. I would like to propose another approach.

One fundamental characteristic of a successful school is that it is able to gather, systematically and consistently, information on the expectations and perceptions of all parts of its community and to act intelligently on that information.

In this country we do not have an education service which values self-evaluation for what it is: a reflective approach by the institution itself to the changing needs of those that participate within it.

The chief inspector is on record as criticising certain teacher organisations for supporting self-evaluation as an alternative to the current model of inspection. The Government has cautiously moved towards schools setting their own targets, but purely in the area of core subject outcomes.

Yet, in Scotland the Scottish Inspectorate not only uses performance indicator and relative rating criteria when inspecting schools, but also evaluates each school's own ethos indicators, indicators which have been arrived at by the self-evaluation process.

It is no accident that the Scottish inspection system is relatively uncontroversial and is supported by teachers. Remarkable things have happened in Scotland, although I suspect Michael Forsythe is still eyeing the terrain with ideas of fundamental change and with a view towards moving the Scottish evaluation model towards that which exists in England and Wales.

Nevertheless it would be unthinkable in England for local education authorities, a university research department and the government department responsible for education to produce collaboratively a model for inspection.

Some of you may know that recently the NUT commissioned Professor John MacBeath from the Quality in Education Centre at the University of Strathclyde to, and I quote:

- 'examine the value and scope of school self-evaluation and its relationship to external evaluation;

- consider to what extent the model developed in Scottish schools might provide useful insights to support development work in England and Wales;

- develop, in partnership with schools, a user-friendly but rigorous framework for school self-evaluation;

- identify what part teachers, pupils, parents, governing bodies and other groups could play in the process of self-evaluation.'

The research was extremely successful. The report comprised an ethnographic study of the schools in the research, a set of practical instruments for self-evaluation and an alternative model for inspection. Entitled *Schools Speak for Themselves* (Macbeath et al., 1996) it has gained enormous support both from LEAs and schools. Indeed over 25 local education authorities are using the report as the basis for their professional development programmes this year.

The point I want to make is that school self-evaluation is in reality research into what works and doesn't work by institutions for themselves and of themselves.

One of the most illuminating sections of *Schools Speak for Themselves* is entitled 'The Good Teacher'. Children and young people arrive at fascinating distinctions between good and bad teachers. The last paragraph of that section on 'Critical Incident Analysis' makes the obvious link between self-evaluation and processes which can defuse conflict between pupils and staff.

My purpose in dwelling on school self-evaluation is that such an approach if conducted systematically, fairly and thoroughly provides a vital foundation for both managing the behaviour of pupils and for preventative behaviour strategies.

Entitlement for Teachers

It is still a matter of concern that a relatively low priority has been given to training of both student and practising teachers in the psychology of relationships between teachers and pupils. The *Pupils with Problems* (DfEE, 1994) circulars represented a big step forward. However, the first two circulars (8/84 and 9/94) were weighted down with, what one might call, a professional development framework approach rather than one which defined teacher entitlements.

Nevertheless, there were some exceptions, many of which came about as a result of a remarkably open consultative approach by the DfEE towards constructing the circulars. The NUT itself was successful in inserting some critical 'entitlement' statements.

'Teachers should be able to feel that their work to maintain discipline in the class takes place within the framework of the school's overall behaviour policy. The contribution of both teaching and non-teaching staff to the development of a policy on the systems and steps to be taken to resolve a disciplinary crisis, is important.' (DfEE circular 8/94)

and

'Teachers will need to know the range of options open to them, which may involve other members of staff, when a pupil needs to be removed temporarily from the classroom or other action taken. ... If a child does not acquiesce to the punishment, the teacher should feel free to consult a senior member of staff without this being regarded as a failure. It is important in such cases not to allow the child's refusal to escalate into an issue in its own right. Teachers should be able to feel confident that they have support and guidance available when they need it.' (DfEE circular 8/94)

11

and

'Teachers should not be blamed for failures in maintaining good order and discipline if the necessary support systems within the school for providing practical advice and help are absent.' (DfEE circular 8/94)

These points underline what I believe was a genuine shift in the thinking of the DfEE, a shift which has yet to take place in many schools. Teachers can feel isolated and be made to feel failures when faced with difficult pupils. The act of asking for support should not be seen as an admission of failure by the teacher. School behaviour policies, or 'school discipline policies' as they are known under the Education Bill, have very little relevance and will continue to have very little relevance if they do not answer the following questions.

- Do all teachers know who to turn to within the school when they need support?

- Do all staff know and agree that particular pupils can be difficult?

- Where should pupils go if they need to be removed from the classroom?

- What is an acceptable 'cooling off' period for the child and where should that child go to 'cool off'?

- When, as the DfEE puts it in its *Pupil Behaviour and Discipline* circular, might standing a child outside the classroom be 'an appropriate sanction in certain circumstances'?

- Are there flexible arrangements for teachers to be able to ask other teachers to take pupils for short periods of time?

- When can teachers, within directed time, share views about pupils that have particular problems? (John McBeath's 'critical incident analysis')

- What are the arrangements for pupil withdrawal and in-class support? Is there a mixture of both?

These are critical questions.

There is no point in repeating the findings of *Discipline in Schools* (DES,1989) (the Elton Report), but it is worth repeating a recommendation from the summary of the report.

'We see the roles of initial and in-service training as crucial. ... This leads us to make two key recommendations. The first is that all initial teacher training courses should include specific practical training in ways of motivating and managing groups of pupils, and of dealing with those who challenge authority. The second is that similar in-service training should be provided through school based groups. These groups should aim not only to refine classroom management skills, but also to develop patterns of mutual support amongst colleagues.'

In a sense much of that paragraph distils my points made so far. Eight years on, however, there is still difficulty in ensuring that national agencies absorb the impact of those conclusions.

For example, it was left to the DfEE's Working Group on School Security (DfEE, 1996) to secure the agreement of the Teacher Training Agency to identify training in pupil behaviour as a national priority.

'The Teacher Training Agency should give due attention to the importance of training in pastoral care and its implications for pupils' behaviour' (Recommendation 18 of the report of the Working Group on School Security. May 1996).

Restraint, Holding and Touching

Probably the weakest area of current advice to teachers is in the area of physical contact between teachers and pupils. The DfEE was only willing to devote one or two paragraphs in DfEE Circular 9/94 to the issue of physical restraint.

'Desirably, more than one adult should be present (although this is not always possible). Physical restraint is normally necessary only to prevent a pupil causing harm to him or herself or to others, seriously damaging property or committing some criminal act which risks harm to people and to property when verbal commands will not control the behaviour. The purpose of intervention is to restore safety and restraint should not continue for longer than is necessary. Physical contact and restraint should never be used in anger and teachers should seek to avoid any injury to the child. They are not expected to restrain a child if by doing so they will put themselves at risk.'

The DfEE refers to the Department of Health's guidelines entitled *Permissible Forms of Control in Children's Residential Care.* The latter, although helpful, is not generally available to teachers, nor has its advice been made known. For example the Department of Health makes a useful distinction between 'holding' and 'restraint', 'holding' being where 'a child may be successfully diverted from destructive or disruptive behaviour by being led away by the hand, arm or means of an arm around his or her shoulder'. The main distinction between 'holding' and 'physical restraint' is the manner of intervention and degree of force applied. Physical restraint involves a degree of force necessary to prevent a child harming him/herself or property. Holding would 'discourage but in itself would not prevent such action' (by a pupil).

Although DfEE circular 9/94 states that it is necessary for schools to have 'a prescribed written handling policy', it has been left to individual schools and local authorities to write those policies and, in general, to re-invent the wheel. In such a critical aspect of teacher/pupil relations, an area which if mismanaged by teachers can literally threaten their careers or, in extreme instances, threaten imprisonment, this position amounts to dangerous negligence by government.

The Government has now shifted. On 22 January the Secretary of State for Education and Employment tabled an amendment to the Education Bill which, according to her press release, 'would allow teachers to restrain disruptive pupils'. Remarkably the beginning of her press release concentrates on the support the amendment will gain from teachers and their unions.

'This measure is good news for teachers and is, I know, welcomed by the teacher unions. It will confirm and clarify the necessary powers teachers have to stop pupils from harming themselves or others, committing a crime or causing serious disruption.

Teachers already have the power to use reasonable steps to restrain seriously disruptive pupils, but this is not well enough understood. There have been cases of teachers being arrested after intervening to break up a playground fight.

This cannot be right. Teachers are in a unique position, they should be allowed, without fear of prosecution, to use physical restraint where this is necessary to stop pupils from fighting.

Furthermore, if a pupil's behaviour is causing a breakdown in good order and discipline in the classroom, the teacher must, as a last resort, be able to lead that pupil away by the arm without jeopardising his or her teaching career.' (DfEE, 22 January 1997)

14

She commits herself to new guidance arising from the amendment.

'My department will produce guidance to assist teachers in understanding what degree of force they may legitimately use in restraining disruptive pupils. We would intend to consult with the teaching profession and others about the content of that guidance.' (DfEE, 22 January 1997)

The NUT has been urging the Government to adopt such an approach for a long time. However, the amendment fails to distinguish between restraint, touching and holding, and any guidance will have to make such distinctions.

For example 'touching' by a teacher can occur when a child or young person is in a state of distress and needs comforting. Furthermore some teachers are necessarily involved in teaching lessons which involve contact, such as in music and some sports where pupils need physical direction in terms of placing their hands on musical instruments or holding sports equipment.

A number of LEAs provide advice to schools on behaviour policies. We expect LEAs to involve teachers' organisations in the formulation of model advice. Both LEAs and those involved in providing advice and support have started to tackle the particular issues of providing practical guidance which works (e.g. Stockport LEA, 1996; Lund, 1996).

Prior to the Government's announcement that it would require LEAs to formulate 'behaviour plans', the NUT had issued advice to its representatives at LEA level (NUT, 1996). The advice urged LEAs to include within their model advice to schools:

- a description of provision for children outside mainstream schools, including the availability of special schools and pupil referral units;

- suggestions for a whole school behaviour policy which can be adopted for primary, secondary and special schools;

- a contact point at LEA level for schools needing advice on behaviour issues;

- advice to schools on touching, holding and restraining pupils;

- details of in-service training in relation to school behaviour policies and the Children Act.

LEA Behaviour Plans

I want to wrap up a number of issues under this last heading.

I would like to start from an individual case. You may know that two members of the NUT were involved in the recent pupil exclusion case at Manton Primary School in Nottinghamshire.

Briefly, at the end of the summer term 1996 the headteacher of the school excluded a year six child for repeated incidences of bad behaviour. The governing body refused to confirm the exclusion. The union representing the majority of the staff at the school balloted their members on industrial action. As members of the NUT the headteacher and the deputy headteacher were similarly protected by ballot.

In short, all staff at the school were of the view that the child should be moved from the school while the majority of the governing body and the parent concerned were against the child being moved. The conflict was resolved temporarily by the LEA brokering a deal whereby the school paid from its own budget for a teacher to teach the child on an individual basis while the LEA's support services monitored the child's education.

The deal broke down when other parents protested about the use of the school's budget for this purpose. Strike action took place for a short time. The parent subsequently agreed to transfer the child.

There are some critical issues arising from the case:

- Could the authority have been more flexible in its attitude?

- Do exclusion procedures meet the needs of the school community?

- Exactly how much effort should be devoted by a school to meeting the behavioural needs of individual children? What kind of balance should there be in terms of support for children with behavioural difficulties in relation to the educational support needed by other children?

- Does the Government have a role, and what impact have its policies had on the ability of LEAs to intervene where there are crises at school level such as the one that took place at Manton School?

To take the issue of exclusions first, I recall a discussion which took place in the NUT about the position which we should take on the draft DES Circular 15/89 Education Reform Act 1988: *Temporary Exceptions from the National Curriculum* (DES, 1989). The draft circular suggested that the effect of a pupil's behaviour on other pupils could constitute grounds for a direction.

16

The NUT took the view, subsequently confirmed by the then Secretary of State, that the test should be whether the pupil's behaviour prevented the pupil himself or herself from benefitting fully from the National Curriculum.

I think that, on reflection, we were wrong in taking that position. One of the most fascinating findings of *Schools Speak for Themselves* (MacBeath et al., 1995) was that it is children themselves who give the highest priority to safety and order in the classroom and it is they who deeply resent individual children disrupting this order and interrupting their learning.

Those that argue that the individual rights of those pupils who are subject to exclusion are de facto rights which should receive the highest priority, ignore the rights of other children within the school. Pupil exclusion is an equal opportunities issue but one for all the children in a school as well as for the child who may be excluded.

The NUT sought to press this view on Government during the passage of the Education Bill. The Bill now requires the governing body and the LEA, when considering a headteacher's proposal for the exclusion of a pupil, to take into account the interests of staff and other pupils. The NUT pressed for additions to that clause which would have required those bodies to take into account the professional judgement of the headteacher and the efficient and effective operation of the school. The DfEE has indicated that the clause covers those intentions adequately and that guidance will amplify the meaning of the clause.

To argue for this approach is not the same as arguing that pupil exclusions are of little concern. While for those pupils who are excluded and their families the experience of exclusion can be traumatic, the incremental rise in exclusions also suggests deep and worrying strains in the system.

One of the most level-headed accounts of the causes and possible routes to reducing the level of exclusion is the OFSTED report *Exclusions from Secondary Schools* 1995/96. In a few condensed paragraphs the report identifies many of the issues which need resolving.

'Partly because few teachers had received adequate training in behaviour management, many were unsure of the distinction between poor behaviour and behaviour springing from deep-seated emotional disturbance, requiring treatment. Referral to specialist services was often too late or ineffective because the services lacked the resources to cope.'

and

17

'LEAs can contribute effectively to reducing the rate of exclusions by:

(i)   detailed monitoring of exclusions;

(ii) using the data collected to inform dialogue with schools;

(iii) offering advice and ensuring that procedures are properly followed;

(iv) maintaining effective support services;

(v)   providing training.' (OFSTED, 1996)

In concurring with these conclusions I do not, however, believe that they describe a full policy picture. Of those schools deemed by OFSTED to be very good schools, some schools had a relatively high level of pupil exclusions. OFSTED is very tentative about the relationship between school effectiveness and pupil exclusion rates, and they are right to be so.

There is an argument for moving away from considering the rate of pupil exclusions as a principal indicator of school effectiveness. The critical issue is whether the school behaviour and discipline policy and the overall ethos of the school have been arrived at by all sections of the school community. Clear school rules reached by consensus and their consistent and fair application are likely to have the effect of reducing pupil exclusions. However, there may very well be cases where, at certain times, the reverse effect could be demonstrated.

It is axiomatic that exclusion happens at the point at which the institution can no longer provide the education for the child concerned either temporarily or permanently. The critical question in these circumstances is whether an outside body, whether a local authority or another school, could provide the support which would obviate the need for that exclusion. For the NUT, pupil exclusions remains a sensitive issue. The Union itself first raised the issue in 1992 when a survey it conducted of LEAs indicated a 20 per cent rise of temporary and permanent exclusions over two years (NUT, 1994). A recent survey by the NUT of exclusions of black pupils indicated that Afro-Caribbean pupils are over-represented in school exclusions by a factor of 4 (NUT, 1997). The Union recently held a seminar on exclusions of black pupils. It is in no-one's interest, least of all teachers', that a significant group of alienated and rejected pupils develops.

Many LEAs, as the OFSTED report found, are indeed providing behaviour support to schools via behaviour support teams. Indeed it is the resurrection, via GEST, of behaviour support teams which represents a standing criticism of the Government's requirements on local education authorities to delegate at least 90 per cent of their resources to schools.

Undoubtedly LEA support to schools has been severely and fundamentally compromised by LMS requirements. But, the most imaginative authorities are finding ways of providing services to schools, for example, through buy-back arrangements, which can compensate for the removal of such services.

I want to suggest, however, that there are other constraints on the effectiveness of LEAs which are not primarily Government driven. A small number of local education authorities have adopted inclusive education policies. It is too early to determine whether they work, but such policies are almost invariably local authority member driven.

While this presentation is not about the merits or demerits of inclusive education per se, it is worth reflecting on whether inclusive education policies driven by local authority members, particularly in the area of emotional behavioural difficulties, are able to trigger a flexible and pragmatic set of support mechanisms for schools.

Over-rigid LEA policies in relation to emotional difficulties are not the best way of providing support to schools. There is little evidence which indicates that there can be any better approach adopted by an LEA than one of pragmatism in terms of the organisation of its support provision and one of monitoring very carefully the needs of schools within its area. An LEA which adopts a single policy first and then seeks to respond to schools' needs with only one strategy in its armoury is likely to fail in its job.

I would suggest that there is a consensus over many of the pupils' behaviour clauses of the Government's Education Bill. Within my presentation I have not addressed the issue of home/school partnership agreements, largely because they are peripheral to any discussion about pupil behaviour in schools. In short, such agreements represent an ineffective admissions requirement. Since the priority for parents is to secure a place for their child in a school of their choice, the act of signing will be simply one of those steps which have to be taken in order to secure a place.

Government must reflect on its policies. The implications of requiring LEAs to produce behaviour plans are enormous. Support to schools in this area must be seen as a core LEA responsibility, outside the requirements of LMS. A combination of government grants and ring-fenced resources at

LEA level combined with a genuine commitment by LEAs to resolving which forms of support are appropriate for school communities themselves. At least it points in the right direction.

In this respect, for once Government and teacher organisations agree.

'The clause (LEA behaviour plans) requires local education authorities to consult when preparing their plans. Those consulted will include schools, teachers' representatives, parents' representative bodies, other local services (not LEAs), social services departments, any local voluntary bodies and others with general youth interests. Local education authorities will need to take account of the views of all those important local organisations before plans can be finalised.' (Eric Forth - Standing Committee D, 17 December 1996)

A late conversion is better than no conversion at all.

References

DES (1989) *Discipline in Schools*. Report of the Committee of Enquiry chaired by Lord Elton. HMSO.

DES (1989) Circular 15/89 *Education Reform Act 1988: Temporary Exceptions from the National Curriculum*. DES.

DfEE (1994) *Pupils with Problems*. Circulars.

DfEE (1996) Report of the Working Group on School Security.

DfEE (1997) Press Release, *Restraining Disruptive Pupils - Government's amendment to the Education Bill*. 22 January 1997.

Department of Health (1994) *Permissible Forms of Control in Children's Residential Care*.

Hansard (1996) Standing Committee D, 17 December 1996.

Lund, R (1996) *A Whole School Behaviour Policy. A Practical Guide*. Kogan Page.

NUT (1992) *Survey of Pupil Exclusions in LEAs.* Unpublished.

NUT (1996) *Discipline in Schools* - Advice to NUT members. NUT.

NUT (1996) *Schools Speak for Themselves. Towards a Framework for Self-Evaluation.* Quality in Education Centre, University of Strathclyde.

NUT (1997) *Survey of Exclusions of Black Pupils.* Unpublished.

OFSTED (1996) *Exclusions from Secondary Schools* - 1995/96.

Stockport Metropolitan Borough Council Education Division (1996) *Care and Control.* Unpublished.

Policy in a World of Emotions: Where to now with EBD?

PETER GRAY

Summary

This paper sets out to explore the particular policy issues that surround provision for pupils with emotional and behavioural difficulties (EBD). It also considers the range of policy options that are available to decision-makers and assesses their strengths and weaknesses, and includes some personal views about 'best bets' for the future. It starts from the premise that local authorities have a key role to play in planning strategically to meet the needs of pupils with EBD.

EBD: The nature of the area

The issue of EBD has recently acquired a greater significance compared with many other areas of SEN. Schools, local authorities, and government departments all seem to be struggling to identify coherent and positive ways forward. Moreover, there is a worrying and growing separation of EBD from consideration of SEN issues in general, with a resurgence in public discussion of concepts such as 'unteachable' which formally disappeared from the education vocabulary with the 1944 Education Act and had not even been applied to those children with the most significant learning disabilities since 1970.

In this context, it is particularly important that policy issues are looked at calmly and analytically. Herein lies a major problem. Difficult behaviour in children provides a strong challenge to adults' sense of their own personal effectiveness. This feature applies whether we are parents, teachers, head-teachers, local authority administrators, members of support agencies or even politicians. We can all feel under pressure at times to provide a 'robust response'.

It is true that achieving positive change in children's behaviour and self-esteem can also be one of the most rewarding experiences for those who teach, care for, or in any way feel responsible for them. However, lack of progress can as easily lead to defensiveness and blame, and can work against the development of effective collaboration and shared responsibility for finding ways forward.

At a policy level, the pressure for immediate solutions can also lead to poorly thought out and 'ad hoc' responses which may have some short-term symbolic or political benefit, but do little to help secure longer-term improvement. An analogy would be with penal policy where there can be

22

pressure for more and longer custodial sentences without regard to their effectiveness in cutting crime.

The emotive nature of the EBD area significantly affects our capacity to achieve clear answers to key policy questions such as 'What is EBD and what is its extent and severity?'; 'How do we know whether things are getting worse or better?'; 'Who is the client towards whom policy should be directed?'. Consideration of the issues around each of these areas is the focus of the following section.

EBD: Key policy issues:
(a) Problem definition and quantification:

Planning responses to EBD requires some understanding of its level and range. The emotional experience and subjectivity of 'EBD-ness' makes this extremely difficult to achieve. Those LEAs, for example, that have attempted to introduce 'pupil audit' systems as a basis for quantifying and resourcing SEN have found the EBD area most difficult to define and moderate.

Concepts such as the 'Warnock 20%' have been helpful in reinforcing the notion that pupils with EBD are a matter for all teachers and schools and not just for 'specialists'. However, they also carry the risk of differentiating much larger groups of children than might be included by more conservative definitions. Moreover, the EBD label gives rise to much more negative consequences for the pupils concerned than some other descriptors of special educational needs.

It is quite clear that, despite the broad emphasis on a 'continuum of EBD' (mirroring the continuum of SEN described by Warnock), there are considerable confusions in practice around such issues as 'Do all children with EBD have SEN? Aren't some just disruptive ... or plain evil?', 'Isn't there a difference between disruptive pupils and those who are 'disturbed' or whose problems have some medical causation?', 'Isn't most EBD really to do with pupil disaffection with the curriculum and the life opportunities on offer?'. Many of these issues relate to views about causation which again vary considerably between teachers, schools, parents, and indeed support agencies, administrators and politicians. They also reflect the fact that EBD is essentially a socially constructed phenomenon.

Differing views about definition inevitably affect decisions and views about priorities and the focus for energy and resources. And these are further complicated by the tendency of those on the 'inside' of schools to attribute EBD problems to outside causes (e.g. child factors, parents, society

23

at large (Cross & Moses, 1985) and those on the 'outside' to see things more in terms of factors which schools themselves contribute (Rutter et al., 1979; Reynolds, 1985; HMI, 1996).

(b) Assessing change and evaluating progress:

Policy-makers have continually reported that pupil behaviour is getting worse. Moral panics about the state of behaviour in schools have led to a succession of government-commissioned reports (Hadow, 1927; Elton, 1989) to examine what should be done to halt a further perceived decline from the 'golden age'. And yet, those historians who have sought documentary or oral evidence of the nature of behaviour in previous generations question whether such a golden age ever existed (Humphries, 1981; Gardner, 1996).

The strong tendency of society to romanticise the past, together with the subjective definition of 'EBD-ness', leaves policy-makers with little chance of clearly gauging any deterioration or improvement. True, there is now more objective information on national levels of permanent exclusion (Parsons & Howlett, 1996), which suggests a significant deterioration. But, are we certain that this represents a change in pupil behaviour as opposed to a shift in expectations? And while there are plenty of factors that might explain an increase in EBD (e.g. increasing poverty/unemployment, social/family changes, earlier puberty, reduced public respect for teacher authority, curriculum restrictions, reducing school budgets/increasing class sizes), how can we tell which of these are crucial?

Conversely, how can we ensure that we recognise and acknowledge relative improvement? EBD is generally not an area that people feel confident or good about, and it is therefore not unknown for relatively successful initiatives to be overtaken by political reactions to renewed pressure for 'decisive action'.

(c) Responding to different interests:

EBD is a social issue and inevitably policy has to take account of a range of interests. These often conflict and can be difficult to reconcile in practice. There have also been significant shifts in emphasis over the last 20 years along a number of key dimensions:

(i) individual rights vs collective responsibility:

Margaret Thatcher's comment 'There's no such thing as society' marked a move towards a culture of greater individualism in the early 1980s. The individual was portrayed as fettered by excessive state control and interference, with choices limited by restrictions in the free market and by various forms of 'social engineering'. The politics of the Tory Government of this period, which captured the popular mood, reasserted the individual as supreme, with greater power and choice as a consumer of both private and public services, and enhanced rights, particularly with regard to public sector organisations.

In the area of education, this trend has focused on parents as consumers, having choice of schools for their children and entitlements to information, influence, and to particular standards of local authority service. With regard to EBD in particular, it has gone in two potentially opposing directions: an increased capacity for parents of 'other children' to influence schools' tolerance of pupils who may interfere with their children's learning; and increased legal rights of parents of children with EBD to influence professional decision-making about exclusion or alternative school placement.

This emphasis has tended to discourage collective responsibility among parents for the good of all children in the school community. While many schools and LEAs have sought to uphold this kind of ethos, they have found themselves downgraded by successive legislation from a position of moral leadership to mere providers of services.

(ii) **teachers' rights vs. the rights of parents and children:**
It is not just the rights of parents that have become more significant over the last 20 years. In addition, the rights of children themselves have achieved a much greater prominence. This has been partly due to the greater profile given to child protection as a result of notorious cases of family and of institutional abuse. There has also been a significant international movement towards defining and documenting the particular rights of children.

While this implies that the rights of 'other pupils' cannot be ignored, it has meant considerable emphasis on good quality assessment and planning for troubled young people, with their individual needs being more carefully considered. In both education and care planning, systems are increasingly in place to avoid pragmatic and 'ad hoc' short-term responses that may have an adverse effect on longer-term outcomes. There is also more emphasis placed on exploring the full range of mainstream school and community-based solutions.

Approaches that focus on the rights and entitlements of children and parents, including those that schools find difficult to teach or negotiate with, inevitably present some challenge to teachers' sense of authority. These approaches also place a greater emphasis on teacher responsibility, with difficult pupil behaviour seen as a product of poor school management or teaching unless proved otherwise. It is perhaps for this reason that teachers themselves, who feel laden with ever-increasing responsibility, have started to assert their own individual rights, for example not to teach pupils they consider to be a physical threat to their own safety. Teacher union involvement in recent high profile cases has been evident on this theme. While the legal framework on exclusions offers a means by which parent and child rights can be taken into account, teachers are now arguing that their rights should be recognised too. In addition, they are arguing that the responsibilities, as well as the rights, of other parties (e.g. parents) should be properly identified. Both major political parties have recently reacted to this call through the notion of home-school contracts.

Balancing the rights and responsibilities of teachers, pupils and parents is a major issue in policy and provision for EBD. It is also one where an 'individual rights' approach does not tend to achieve a positive resolution. LEA officers who have a legal duty to review all permanent exclusions are currently at the centre of this issue. While legislation prescribes active consideration of pupil and parent rights and entitlements, there is increasing pressure on them from schools to give priority to the teacher perspective, either through implied threats of industrial action or school withdrawal from LEA control.

(iii) punishment vs welfare:

Until relatively recently, it has tended to be assumed that young people (at least those below the age of criminal responsibility) present behaviour difficulties because of circumstances beyond their control. 'Welfare' has therefore been seen to be a more appropriate response than punishment. Cases such as Jamie Bulger have led the public to question these assumptions, and punitive approaches are now being proposed for increasingly younger children. It has become difficult for some teachers and schools to be persuaded that EBD should be regarded as a special educational need or given the same supportive and careful attention that the *Code of Practice* (SEN) currently describes. And, there is evidence that this shift in attitude is occurring not just in mainstream schools but in special schools for pupils with severe learning difficulties where permanent exclusion levels are also rising significantly (Male, 1996).

I am not suggesting here that teachers, or society more generally, are becoming more interested in punishment for the sake of it. However, there is a noticeable shift in emphasis away from the priority that needs to be given to accepting and responding to our most troubled young people and towards safeguarding the needs and wants of 'the other pupils', their parents and the teachers who want to teach them. While this approach currently appears to have some 'natural justice', its costs (both financial and social) are at risk of being significantly undervalued.

Policy options for EBD:
I have attempted in the first part of this paper to portray the context in which policy options for EBD have to be considered. The next section considers the range of options available to schools and LEAs, and some of their strengths and weaknesses.

So what would you do with a million pounds?

Most commentators would argue that the 'EBD problem' has worsened since education budgets in schools and LEAs have become increasingly under pressure.

A salutary question in this context is 'If additional money for EBD could now be found, what should it be spent on?'. As an example, if all primary schools were to receive an additional £10,000 in their annual budget share, should this be spent on:

(a) increasing teaching staff to help reduce class sizes?

(b recruiting a non-teaching assistant to provide in-class support or withdrawal?

(c) buying more support service time?

(d) paying for a major programme of consultancy/training/staff development?

(e) buying one place in a new off-site unit (which once occupied would use up the school's full £10,000 allocation until vacated)?

(f) offering more pre-school experience to prevent later problems?

27

In considering these options, we might say 'all of them'. Typically, however, schools and LEAs have to make choices within a limited budget and priorities need to be established. While the notion of a 'continuum of provision' is an attractive one, it is now less possible for us to have everything!

One approach adopted by some LEAs has been to maximise delegation of all SEN funds to schools so that they can make local decisions appropriate to their particular needs. This permits a variety of different responses. While this approach is attractive, it has a number of problems in relation to EBD:

(i) it is difficult to establish a reliable and simple formula by which funds for EBD can be distributed. While most people would acknowledge between-school differences in the incidence of pupils with EBD, it is extremely difficult to quantify these because of the definitional problems outlined above. Proxy indicators (e.g. social disadvantage measures) are relevant, but are insensitive to individual cases of extreme need.

(ii) some forms of provision are only really viable if they serve a number of different schools. There are benefits therefore in not desegregating funds to the individual school level when cluster approaches are feasible (Dyson & Gains, 1993).

(iii) schools retain a legal power to exclude permanently. Without precise targeting of funds to particular pupils, it can be extremely difficult for LEAs to remove resources from schools at the point of permanent exclusion in order that they can make suitable alternative provision.

(iv) LEAs have a duty under the 1993 Education Act to provide for permanently excluded pupils. They therefore have more than a passing interest in the effectiveness of a school's response. LEAs still need to have an informed view about what approaches are most likely to achieve relative success. Delegation itself cannot be seen as a solution.

So what is the range of options available?
Off-site provision:
Topping (1983) and others have identified a hierarchy of EBD provision which includes a range of off-site options from the most to least expensive.

Some young people, for example, currently experience 52 week provision in residential schools or long-term care establishments. This can be extremely expensive (£80,000 per year is not unusual). Outcomes in such cases are not convincing, although for some pupils at considerable educational, domestic and neighbourhood risk, there does not seem to be an alternative option.

This type of provision becomes less expensive as we progress through termly and weekly residential to day EBD special schools, and more cost-effective as provision is able to respond more flexibly to changing needs. Thus, most Pupil Referral Units (PRUs), with less statutorily defined admission policies and the option of part-time attendance, can provide more flexibly than special schools.

The off-site option is clearly attractive to mainstream schools and others who see the removal of a very difficult pupil as providing significant relief. This kind of provision, however, is not cost-effective and can never be available to more than a very small minority of children. While part-time and short-term placements are less expensive and potentially more accessible, they are typically less successful than we might predict in getting pupils back full-time into mainstream school. Once a pupil leaves mainstream provision for any period, his/her return has to be very carefully planned to be successful and this can often require considerable additional support (Gray & Noakes, 1993).

Topping's 1983 review of off-site provision indicated that outcomes for pupils at that time were not particularly positive. Since then, there has been clear evidence from a succession of HMI reports that pupils in day EBD special schools and units tend to experience considerable social and curricular deprivation. The DfEE guidance on PRUs (Circ 11/94) and the more recent OFSTED framework seek to address this problem. However, there are many real issues that arise from grouping extremely difficult pupils together, and from having to balance teaching, therapy and containment, which mean off-site establishments of this kind have inherent problems.

On-site options:

Some of the social and curricular problems identified above can be addressed where specialist EBD facilities are 'on-site' in a mainstream school. This kind of provision can also be cheaper because of greater flexibility in staffing and material costs. There is some evidence too of better outcomes from on-site compared to off-site provision (Galloway & Goodwin, 1987).

On-site facilities, however, present a number of policy difficulties. Firstly, LEAs can rarely afford to fund such facilities for individual mainstream schools to provide solely for their own EBD pupils. On-site units, therefore, are typically area provisions. In a climate where schools are more concerned about their public image, this makes such an option less attractive for potential 'host' schools. This is particularly the case at secondary school level where EBD problems are apparently more severe. Secondly, the more integrated the on-site facility is within the host school, the more likely it is that its focus drifts away from the 'most difficult' pupils towards 'more deserving' and less needy groups. Individual outcome studies (e.g. Bell & Colbeck, 1989) suggest that on-site facilities are rarely totally inclusive, with some of their population typically being excluded or transferred to other forms of specialist provision. Finally, while on-site provision may seem more palatable than more segregated options (and therefore more popular in terms of placement), there are genuine questions about whether outcomes would be any different if pupils had remained supported in their own local mainstream school.

Curriculum approaches:

It has been argued that a significant amount of EBD derives from pupil disaffection with a restrictive and irrelevant curriculum (Booth & Coulby, 1987). Teachers themselves have suggested that the introduction of a more prescribed National Curriculum has given them less room to manoeuvre creatively with pupils for whom formal learning may not be the priority. Curriculum modification and differentiation continue to be major elements of any recommended response to pupils with SEN. However, there is evidence of more substantial attempts to respond to EBD through alternative curricula, particularly at Key Stage 4 where National Curriculum requirements have been somewhat relaxed following the Dearing review.

In exploring different curriculum approaches, there is also evidence of increasing acceptance of pupils venturing beyond the school gates for curriculum access. Numbers of 14+ pupils attending FE Colleges, for example, are rising nationally and there is evidence of participation of pupils with EBD in a range of 'alternative opportunities' off-site while remaining on the main school roll.

While this kind of development has its attractions, there are major issues around ensuring pupil attendance and quality of educational opportunity. LEAs themselves have such responsibilities for permanently excluded pupils. However, for pupils on the roll of mainstream schools, there may not be sufficient safeguards at present to ensure proper educational access.

Even with better safeguards, there are very real dangers of creating a growing underclass of pupils who have significantly reduced educational entitlements.

Training:
A range of good quality training packages are now available (e.g. Galvin, Mercer & Costa, 1990). The best of these include material to assist the development of effective approaches at whole school, classroom and individual pupil levels. For hard-pressed teachers, time to reflect on practice and share experiences with colleagues remains a powerful opportunity for development and mutual support. And this is vital to maintain motivation in an area where teachers can feel exposed and isolated (Miller, 1996).

A key problem in this area is that, while such training is popular, it can bypass the issues presented by the most difficult and challenging pupils, with a common response being 'Well, it was useful for most kids but not this one!'. Some more recent developments such as *Circles of Friends* (Newton et al., 1996) can be of help by targeting more explicitly the needs of the most difficult pupils, while also demonstrating benefits to other children and to the development of a positive school ethos.

Projects and multi-disciplinary approaches:
This has been a significant growth area in recent years. Not only has the DfEE continued to supply funds on a one-year basis through its 'Truancy and Disaffection' GEST category, but the area of youth disaffection has also attracted interest from a range of other voluntary sector, private and government-funded bodies. The overall amount of project funding now available is breathtaking, but so too is the breadth of funding sources and the potential for confusion and duplication of effort. LEAs, who could play a more central part in project coordination, are now only one player in an open market where every project provider is eager to demonstrate its immediate worth and there is little independent evaluation of longer-term benefits.

The other major issue with project approaches is that their duration is often uncertain. In this context, schools and LEAs remain unclear how far the focus of projects should be developmental (and assume no longer-term continuation of project funds) or supplementary (in the hope that funding from some source can be sustained). The lack of predictable longer-term funding means that the learning achieved through some apparently successful projects can be wasted.

Renewed energy is currently being directed at establishing more coherent multi-disciplinary responses to the EBD problem. These have increasingly involved the Education departments working together with Social Services departments, the youth services and sometimes with local health authorities, to achieve more coordinated outcomes for children and families regarded as at risk. This is clearly an important and worthwhile aim, as there are dangers of agencies undermining each other or duplicating effort. However, it does not replace the need for different agencies to ensure effective outcomes in their own area of responsibility. And, it does require effective collaboration at the mundane level of casework, not just at the more exotic end of managerial liaison and project coordination.

Support service responses:
The effectiveness of support services has come increasingly under fire from various quarters. On the one hand, they are accused of de-skilling mainstream colleagues (Goodwin, 1983), and on the other, of inhibiting more flexible and appropriate school-based responses (Thomas, 1996). In the area of EBD, there has been a significant problem nationally in the development of EBD support services. These have typically been born out of progressive rationalisation of a disparate range of alternative provision. EBD support teachers have often been asked to take on the complex and challenging role of supporting pupils and teachers in mainstream schools, which requires different skills to those needed for direct teaching of difficult young people. Very little recognised training has been available to help them make this transition.

However, there is evidence of significantly successful support service work in the EBD area (e.g. Crombie & Noakes, 1992). Services usually work best when linked closely to other relevant support agencies (e.g. educational psychologists, education welfare officers). They work most effectively when they are able to reduce the level of difficult behaviour presented by individual pupils in mainstream schools, without needing to remove the pupil for significant periods or provide an unrealistic level of additional support which cannot be maintained for more than a short period of time. While this approach may not be as attractive as the off-site placement, it is considerably more cost-effective to both schools and LEAs in the long run.

Cluster initiatives:
A variety of 'cluster' (group of schools) approaches to managing SEN have been described by Dyson and Gains (op cit.). Such approaches range

from shared policies, procedures and training to the pooling and targeting of resources (Cade & Caffyn, 1994). Cluster initiatives in the area of EBD are less common. However, there has been a tradition in some localities for schools to 'exchange' permanently excluded pupils. There have also been some examples of mainstream headteachers playing an active part in managing and reviewing admissions to both on- and off-site units.

As the risk of exclusion becomes greater, it is even more important that pupils with EBD remain 'visible'. It is currently too easy to say 'This child would be better taught by someone else somewhere else' and not to have any responsibility for following up the effects of that decision on the pupil and his/her future teachers. Schools working together can help to define better the pupils most at risk and target resources more effectively towards them. And, a more direct role in managing the full extent of the problem helps schools to understand that there are no easy or cheap solutions to this area. It also helps schools to value more highly the relative successes that are achieved through time-consuming but essential planning and review.

EBD Policy: a few 'best bets':

The final section of this paper offers a personal view of some practical policy steps that could be taken to improve the current situation faced by schools and LEAs. They are in no particular order of priority.

(1) Break down PRU/EBD special school boundaries to ensure that any off-site support can operate as flexibly as possible. There are dangers in seeing PRUs as a 'half-way house' between mainstream and special schools, as the DfEE currently implies. This reinforces a tendency for resources to drift away from the most difficult pupils and towards easier and 'more deserving' cases. The complexity of admission and reintegration arrangements for special schools also reduces their cost-effectiveness in responding to this area of need.

(2) Ensure that EBD support services have adequate training and preparation for their roles. Ensure that the role is more clearly identified as one that should successfully assist mainstream schools to manage pupils confidently and independently. Value EBD support as a skilled and theoretically-based activity rather than simply a matter of intuition and empathy. Ensure all LEA support services linked to EBD are properly coordinated, with effective links between pupil and school development issues.

(3) Define good practice with regard to curriculum provision beyond the mainstream school gates (particularly at Key Stages 3 & 4). Clarify expectations with regard to quality and pupil attendance.

(4) Provide training opportunities for teachers to reflect on the EBD issue away from the classroom and immediate school culture, and to understand the full extent of its social and emotional definition.

(5) Establish an overall mechanism for project coordination (LEAs are still a sensible vehicle). Include support from a steering group made up of broader interests. Ensure that effective multi-disciplinary work is 'normalised' at the local level.

(6) Maximise mainstream school involvement, not just in developing effective approaches to pupil management and in promoting a positive school ethos, but also in those situations where pupils cannot be maintained in the mainstream setting. Existing legislation draws a firm line under mainstream school responsibility at the point of permanent exclusion. Duties at this point transfer entirely to the LEA, in conjunction with parents. Would the attitudes of mainstream schools to permanent exclusion be different if they had more responsibility themselves for the planning and review of alternative school arrangements?

(7) Engage mainstream schools in joint initiatives to develop improved responses to EBD at the local level. There is a range of possibilities when people put their heads together. For example, schools can develop 'family' or cluster policies for the management of difficult behaviour that allow some continuity of approach across different age-phase boundaries. They can work together to reduce the stresses that occur at school transition. In localities, groups of schools can pool resources to develop community projects. And at the individual pupil level, they can be more creative about organising curriculum packages and arranging pupil exchanges if they are able to use each other's resources more flexibly.

(8) Continue to press for better overall funding for education, so that both teachers and pupils have a better chance of resolving problems successfully in the mainstream setting where positive change is most likely to occur.

It has been the purpose of this paper to emphasise that magic solutions in the EBD area are an illusion. There is no real substitute for the hard slog of trying to plan calmly and collaboratively the best way forward, both at the school and individual pupil level. The nature of the policy context described in the first part of this paper, however, confirms that this is not always possible. We are all human after all and the EBD area is about as human as they come!

References

Bell, G H & Colbeck, B (1989) *Experiencing integration: The Sunnyside Action Enquiry Project.* London: Falmer.

Board of Education (1927) *The Education of the Adolescent: Report of the Consultative Committee* (Hadow Report). London.

Booth, T & Coulby, D (Eds.) (1987) *Producing and reducing disaffection.* Milton Keynes: Open University Press.

Cade, L & Caffyn, R (1994) *The King Edward VI family: An example of clustering in Nottinghamshire.* Support for Learning, 9, (2), 83-88.

Croll, P & Moses, D (1985) *One in Five: The assessment and incidence of special educational needs.* London: RKP.

Crombie, R & Noakes, J (1992) *Developing a service to support children with behaviour difficulties in mainstream school.* Educational and Child Psychology, 9, (4), 57-67.

Department for Education (1994) Circular 11/94: *The education by LEAs of children otherwise than at school.*

Department of Education and Science (1989) *Discipline in schools* (the Elton Report). London: HMSO.

Dyson, A & Gains, C (1993) *Special needs and effective learning: Towards a collaborative model for the year 2000.* In *Rethinking special needs in mainstream schools: towards the year 2000.* London: David Fulton.

Galloway, D & Goodwin, C (1987) *The education of disturbing children: pupils with learning and adjustment difficulties.* Harlow: Longman.

Galvin, P, Mercer, S & Costa, P (1990) *Building a Better Behaved School.* Harlow: Longman.

Gardner, P (1996) *The giant at the front: Young teachers and corporal punishment in inter-war elementary schools:* History of Education, 25, (2), 141-163.

Goodwin, C (1983) *The contribution of support services to integration planning.* In T. Booth & P. Potts (Eds.), *Integrating special education.* Oxford: Blackwell.

Gray, P & Noakes, J (1993) *Reintegrating children with challenging behaviour into the mainstream school community.* In A. Miller & D.A. Lane (Eds.), *Silent conspiracies: Scandals and successes in the care and education of young people.* Stoke-on-Trent: Trentham Books.

Gray, P, Miller, A & Noakes, J (Eds.) (1994) *Challenging behaviour in schools: teacher support, practical techniques and policy development.* London: Routledge.

Humphries, S (1981) *Hooligans or Rebels: An oral history of working class childhood and youth 1889-1939.* Oxford: Blackwell.

Male, D (1996) *Who goes to SLD schools? Journal of Applied Research in Intellectual Disabilities,* 9, (4), 307-323.

Miller, A (1996) *Pupil Behaviour and Teacher Culture.* London: Cassell.

Newton, C, Taylor, G & Wilson, D (1996) *Circles of Friends: An inclusive approach to meeting emotional and behavioural needs.* Educational Psychology in Practice, 11, (4), 41-48.

Parsons, C & Howlett, K (1996) *Permanent exclusions from school: A case where society is failing its children:* Support for Learning, 11, (3), 109-112.

Reynolds, D (1985) *Studying school effectiveness* (Ed.). London: Falmer Press.

Rutter, M, Maughan, B, Mortimore, P, Ouston, J & Smith, A (1979) *Fifteen thousand hours: Secondary schools and their effects on pupils.* London: Open Books.

Thomas, G (1995) *Special Needs at risk?* Support for Learning, 10, (3), 104-112.

Topping, K J (1983) *Educational systems for disruptive adolescents.* London: Croom Helm.

Mental Health in the Classroom

G. J. R. RICHARDSON, Consultant in Child, Adolescent and Family Psychiatry, York Health Services NHS Trust

Introduction

Teachers are second only to parents in affecting children's mental health for good or ill. However, most teachers are unconscious of their role as mental health workers. A common understanding of terms such as 'mental health problems', and their integration with the language of other disciplines is therefore required. Otherwise children will suffer, because each agency will define problematic children in terms which give the responsibility for their management to another agency, whereas mental health problems pervade all agencies who deal with children. The need for, and the problems associated with, the integration of agencies' working have already been eloquently discussed from 'a clear educational perspective' in a previous paper in this series (Dessent, 1996).

The integrated working of all agencies involved with children and young people with mental health problems was at the core of *Together We Stand: The commissioning, role and management of child and adolescent mental health services* (NHS Health Advisory Service, 1995). In that document mental health was defined as:

'The ability to develop psychologically, emotionally, intellectually and spiritually. The ability to initiate, develop and sustain mutually satisfying personal relationships. The ability to become aware of others and to empathise with them. The ability to use psychological distress as a developmental process, so that it does not hinder or impair further development.'

Teachers contribute substantially in all these areas.

It is then possible to move on to define a mental health problem as one which : 'may arise from a young person's difficulties in coping with life, developmental difficulty, the impact of sensory handicap or an educational difficulty or from social difficulties'. Such problems are probably synonymous with the educational term 'emotionally and behaviourally disturbed', one group of those with special educational needs. Not all children with special educational needs will have mental health problems, but they will be vulnerable to them. With the integration of children with special needs into mainstream schools, support networks for their mental health needs must also be integrated into the classroom (Howlin, 1994).

Mental health problems are caused by, and present in, the child's constitutional functioning and in all areas of his/her interaction with his/her environment. It is, therefore, parents and teachers who have the major roles to play in the maintenance of mental health. Other professionals such as child minders, health visitors or social workers follow considerably further behind, although they can be very useful in the early identification of mental health problems and in managing them once identified. Education, Social Services and Health must work together, for children's mental health needs cannot be subdivided into these agencies' discreet areas without similarly dismembering the child.

The psychiatric profession, which provides only an infinitesimal part of the mental health care of children, classifies the more serious mental health problems as mental disorders, defined in the tenth International Classification of Diseases (WHO, 1992) as : 'implying the existence of a clinically recognisable set of symptoms or behaviours associated in most cases with distress and with interference with personal functions'.

These disorders are only a small proportion of the mental health problems produced by constitutional factors, family, educational, social and environmental difficulties, as well as those caused by illness or developmental delay, all of which may impair future psychological functioning. Interestingly the more severe disorders, such as the pervasive developmental disorders, are managed largely by educational interventions, with psychological components such as behaviour modification.

Where are we now?
For the past 30 years it has been recognised that teachers 'in marking work, assessing personality, streaming, setting and selection … are determining the whole future of the child, not only his success in school', and as a result 'The teacher may be subject to impossible demands, being required to ensure success regardless of ability, and having his ability as a teacher criticized on non-educational grounds' (Shipman, 1968).

A major step forward in determining which factors improved a school's effect on young people's mental health was the publication of *Fifteen Thousand Hours* (Rutter, Maughan & Ouston, 1979). Every pupil now leaving school could have benefitted from this work, but political and economic dogma and expediency are the uninvited guests who prevent children from being enriched by research. The fact that schooling affects all areas of a child's functioning, that is his/her mental health, seems now to be generally accepted and is helpfully explained in books for the lay public (Skynner & Cleese, 1994), as well as in publications directed at teachers (*Young Minds*, 1996). The important positive factors required to make a school effective have recently been described by Mortimore (Mortimore, 1995).

However the place of mental health work in school is not universally acknowledged. It is viewed as cataclysmically damaging by some (Citizens Commission on Human Rights, 1995) and apparently ignored by others; the Audit Commission report *Getting in on the Act* (Audit Commission, 1992) made no reference to other agencies who might be working with children with special educational needs, and did not address the difficulties of crossing departmental and institutional boundaries in the interests of the child.

In developing countries, the effects of pressures to achieve academically on the mental health of pupils is well recognised (Bartlet, 1996).

Where do we want to go?
The Teacher as Mental Health Worker
The NHS Health Advisory Service Report (NHS, 1995) proposed that child and adolescent mental health services (CAMHS) could be viewed as operating in four tiers.

Tier 1 services are those provided by professionals with whom children and adolescents with mental health problems first come into contact, e.g. general practitioners, health visitors, social workers and, for every child, teachers. The model recognises the support, training and consultation that these direct contact professionals require from CAMHS.

Tier 2 involves child and adolescent mental health professionals, such as psychiatrists, clinical psychologists or community psychiatric nurses, working on their own with young people who have mental health problems and with their families.

Tier 3 describes the work of mental health professionals in specific specialised teams, such as a family therapy team or an eating disorders team, established to deal with problems which cannot be dealt with by one professional working alone.

At **Tier 4** are those highly specialised services, such as inpatient units and certain very specialised outpatient or liaison services, which are used very infrequently and are usually expensive, their paucity meaning they are not locality based.

Education services could be considered in a similar tiered fashion. Teachers working in the classroom would constitute Tier 1, children requiring special input, possibly at Code of Practice Stages 2 and 3 being at Tier 2. Stage 5 of the Code would correspond to Tier 3, for children whose special educational needs required a team assessment and management, and to Tier 4 for children needing special provision at residential schools.

The most important functional requirement of these models is the easy movement of children and expertise between tiers and between agencies. Supporting teachers as mental health workers therefore becomes a core task of CAMHS. When teachers run into difficulties CAMHS should be able to support them so that they are truly able to bridge the divide between cognitive and social development (Dunn, 1996) in the interests of the mental health of pupils.

Appropriate use of resources

Child and adolescent mental health professionals are not primarily educationalists, and have a limited contribution to make in decisions about usage of appropriate special educational stages. However, a child who requires a Statement at Stage 5 is unlikely not to have mental health problems. Similarly, child and adolescent mental health professionals should have useful contributions to make in the management of a young person with emotional and behavioural difficulties. Again, the integration of services is essential so that child and adolescent mental health professionals working with teachers at Code of Practice Stage 1 will know of the pupils with mental health problems, and may contribute to decisions about placement in other stages. Equally importantly they will know the education professionals, so making for ease of discourse.

What are the obstacles?

The referral system and other perverse incentives 'In the beginning was the word, and the word was anxiety' (Masserman, 1955). The common factor behind all referrals to CAMHS or to a pupil support service is the anxiety of the referrer. If this is understood and addressed it is more likely that confidence will be given to the referrer and hence to the person who is engendering their anxiety. Referrals to other agencies or personnel relieve anxiety but also absolve responsibility, which means a loss of skills delivered to the child, the loss of a relationship and the stigmatising of the child.

The process of 'statementing' also encourages the process of referral to capture extra resources. However the *Code of Practice on the Identification*

41

and Assessment of Special Educational Needs (DfE, 1994) goes some way in trying to stage input for the child so that both the child and the teacher are supported in meeting the child's educational needs. Unfortunately financial constraints mean a process not unlike referral has to take place for a child to move from one stage to another. At Stages 4 or 5 the involvement of other child care professionals and the clear recognition that child and adolescent mental health advice may be required should encourage integration of services rather than referrals between services.

The ignorance of the involvement of other agencies
    The referral system encourages children being moved within agencies but not across them. General practitioners may not be aware that the education support services or social services are involved with a child they refer to CAMHS. The agencies may then be working in ignorance of each other's input, so confusing the family, possibly contradicting each other, and multiplying resource use.

The funding of Health Services
    Health services are increasingly dependent on General Practitioner Fundholders, who only pay for what they refer to specialised services, so many CAMHS have to give higher priority to responding to GP referrals rather than to a request for support in working with a young person in school.
    The other source of funding is from health authorities for whom child and adolescent mental health services are a minuscule responsibility. Ill-informed health authorities are increasingly reluctant to take on requests for service by other agencies such as social services, the courts or the education authority, although some are taking these matters seriously.

Confidentiality
    When discussing individual children, who have special educational needs and who are known to CAMHS, issues of confidentiality arise (Russell, 1996). Local authorities should recognise their obligations concerning confidentiality (DHSS, 1987), although those are more clearly defined when looking at child protection issues rather than issues of educational need (Richardson & Harris-Hendricks, 1996).
    The advantage of supporting teaching staff through consultation is that it avoids children becoming identified patients of the mental health services and hence the confidentiality issues are avoided.

Resources

An area with a population of 250,000 may have two child and adolescent psychiatrists, two clinical psychologists, a psychotherapist and possibly three community psychiatric nurses. The question arises as to whether eight staff can effectively integrate with ten secondary schools, the feeder primary schools and the pupil support services, as well as deal with all other demands on their time.

Poor management of CAMHS

In 1995 the Department of Health commissioned a report on the current status of child and adolescent mental health services (Kurtz, Thornes, & Wolkind, 1994). The report revealed poorly integrated and organised CAMHS within England and Wales. These findings were confirmed in the field visits undertaken for the NHS Health Advisory Service report (NHS, 1995).

The effectiveness of interventions

Kolvin's team studied four different school interventions with children and young people with mental health problems (Kolvin et al., 1981). There was improvement in all intervention groups with some interventions being more effective than others. The resource input was large. Interestingly the consultation interventions, where the pupils had least contact with the outside mental health professional, were the least effective. This is worrying if a consultation and support model is to be promulgated.

The reluctance to manage difficult children

The pressure on teachers to deal with children with special educational needs in large classes is increasing. Teachers understandably resent this and are not well motivated to put extra effort into the management of difficult children, especially if the outcomes of such interventions show up in years rather than hours. The result is often the Pontius Pilate quotation 'We have procedures in school for dealing with misbehaviour yet X desperately needs the sort of help that we cannot provide'. Whereas the more honest statement is 'X is beyond our understanding and control, and we are desperate to be supported in helping him with his difficulties in school'. Non-stigmatising interventions based on current relationships arise from the confidence of the teacher that they have appropriate support. Techniques for managing children with emotional and behavioural difficulties in the classroom have been described (Howlin, 1994), but there are considerable barriers to implementing them.

43

The stigma of mental health

In the early sixteenth century Sir Thomas Elyot wrote in *The Boke Named the Governor*, 'Lorde God, howe many good and clene wittes of children, be nowe a dayes perisshed by ignorant schole maisters'. Education was still stigmatised by Mark Twain in *The Facts Concerning My Recent Resignation*, 'Soap and education are not as sudden as a massacre, but they are more deadly in the long run'. Education has been rehabilitated but mental health remains tainted with madness to pupils' families and teachers. Overcoming such stigma will have to precede effective mental health work within the classroom.

How do we get there?

Around the same time as the NHS Health Advisory Service produced the results of its thematic review of CAMHS (NHS, 1995), the Department for Education introduced guidance on the identification and assessment of children who have educational difficulties which often affect their mental health (DfE, 1994). Similarly the need for child mental health agencies to work closely with the social services departments of local authorities was highlighted (DoH, BMA, Conference of Medical Royal Colleges, 1994). Hence there appears to be some departmental recognition that CAMHS need to work with these other agencies in an integrated manner.

There is also an increasing recognition in the health service that CAMHS must be geared to addressing the needs of local children and their families, and then be properly organised and targeted.

A Locality Child Mental Health Co-ordinator

To overcome children being parcelled as referrals, child and adolescent mental health professionals require close relationships with schools and their support agencies. In view of the paucity of child and adolescent mental health professionals, the role of a locality based child mental health co-ordinator has been postulated. Such a person would have a relationship with local schools, health agencies and social services in order to be aware of all agencies' involvement with young people, and could co-ordinate their involvement by liaison with them. This role may have been initiated in the special needs co-ordinator but will need to be expanded considerably for the person to acquire the necessary local knowledge of child care agencies and to command the respect of local professionals, especially if they provided the only filter into Tiers 2, 3 and 4 of CAMHS. They are also likely to be seen as a source of advice, and so start to take on the primary mental health worker role suggested in *Together We Stand* (NHS, 1995).

Consultation Services

Consultation to agencies working with children is a well recognised aspect of child and adolescent mental health practice. However such services require proper targeting, knowledge and resourcing to be effective (Nicol, 1994).

Teacher Training

The importance of the role of the school and the teacher in the development of the pupil's mental health is not well covered in teacher training. This is an issue which teachers' trainers need to take on.

Conclusion

Children's health depends on their physical and mental well-being. Schools have a large part to play in developing that mental well-being, on which their pupil's current and future psychological functioning will be based. Child and adolescent mental health professionals have an absolute obligation to assist teachers in that work, but considerable work is to be done before teachers view child and adolescent mental health professionals as supportive colleagues rather than psychic wizards or work-shy cranks.

References

Audit Commission (1992) *Getting in on the Act, Provision for Pupils with Special Educational Needs:* the National Picture. HMSO.

Bartlet, L B (1996) *School pressures and child mental health in Afro-Asian countries.* Psychiatric Bulletin, 20, 301-303.

Citizens Commission on Human Rights (1995) *Psychiatry: Education's Ruin.* CCHR International.

Department for Education (1994) *Code of practice on the identification and assessment of special educational needs.* Central Office of Information.

Department of Health and Social Security (1987) *Subject Access to Personal Health Information.* LAC (87) 10 HC. London: HMSO.

Department of Health, British Medical Association, Conference of Medical Royal Colleges (1994) *Child Protection: Medical Responsibilities.* London: Department of Health.

Dessent,T (1996) *Meeting Special Educational Needs - Options for Partnership between Health, Social and Education Services.* The National Association for Special Educational Needs.

Dunn, J (1996) *Children's relationships: Bridging the divide between cognitive and social development.* Journal of Child Psychology and Psychiatry, 37, 507-518.

Howlin, P (1994) *Special educational treatment.* In M. Rutter, E. Taylor, & L. Hersov (Eds.), *Child and Adolescent Psychiatry: Modern Approaches.* Blackwell, 1071-1088.

Kolvin, I, Garside, R F, Nicol, A R, MacMillan, A, Wolstenholme, F & Leitch, I M (1981) *Help Starts Here - The maladjusted child in the ordinary school.* Tavistock Publications.

Kurtz, Z, Thornes, R & Wolkind, S (1994) *Services for the mental health of children and young people in England: A national review.* London: Maudsley Hospital and South Thames (West) Regional Health Authority; 1994.

Masserman, J H (1955) *The Practice of Dynamic Psychiatry.* London: W. B. Saunders.

Mortimore, P (1995) *The positive effects of schooling.* In M. Rutter (Ed.), Psychosocial Disturbances in Young People. Cambridge University Press, 333-364.

NHS Health Advisory Service (1995) *Together We Stand: The Commissioning, Role and Management of Child and Adolescent Mental Health Services.* HMSO.

Nicol, A R (1994) *Practice in nonmedical settings.* In M. Rutter, E. Taylor & L. Hersov (Eds.), *Child and Adolescent Psychiatry: Modern Approaches.* Blackwell, 1040-1054.

Richardson, G & Harris-Hendricks, J (1996) *Confidentiality, consent and the courts.* In J. Harris-Hendriks & M. Black (Eds.), *Child and Adolescent Psychiatry - a New Century.* Royal College of Psychiatrists Occasional Paper OP 33, 40-43.

Russell, P (1996) *Issues arising from the implementation of the Code of Practice on the identification and assessment of Special Educational Needs.* Child Psychology and Psychiatry Review, 1, 110-111.

Rutter, M, Maughan, B, Mortimore, P & Ouston, J (1979) *Fifteen Thousand Hours.* Open Books.

Shipman, M D (1968) *Sociology of the School.* Longman, 13-14.

Skynner, R & Cleese, J (1994) *Life and how to survive it.* Mandarin, 92-93.

World Health Organisation (1992) *The ICD-10 Classification of Mental and Behavioural Disorders.* World Health Organisation, 5.

Young Minds (1996) *Mental Health in Your School: A Guide for Teachers and Schools.* Jessica Kingsley.

Discussion and concluding comments

Notes by CHRIS MARSHALL and PHILIPPA RUSSELL
There were groups and what follows are summaries of their discussions.

Group A

1. What would a quality service look like? It might include preparation for parenthood (in secondary schools). It would start early with a community approach from early childhood onwards to get all agencies involved together (the group noted the current despair concerning present practice but felt there should be a real and collective commitment to attempt to crack the difficulties).

2. Preventative approaches are needed involving parents and families and communities. We need to move towards a situation in which the school system gives more attention to mental health issues and to children's emotional development. Current training crowds out such issues. How can we get mental health professionals helping schools to think about these issues in terms of understanding children's emotional development more effectively? The group also drew attention to the fact that the EBD debate had been hijacked by 'disruptives'and negative images of the 'unteachable child' and 'deserving' and 'undeserving' pupils.

Group B

Group B started by discussing a multi-disciplinary approach, recognising that this could not be considered as a complete panacea (although individuals agreed that multi-disciplinary support was important and with a particular focus could be very effective). Some key issues emerged:

i. Training. Issues about specific training relating to processes which would enable teachers to be more effective rather than dwelling on particular skills. There is a need to evaluate such training and consider outcomes.

ii. There is perhaps a false dichotomy between the National Curriculum and the demands on teachers to teach specific skills - one can be met through the other.

iii.More consideration needed to be given to the extent to which training tries to improve education for all children rather than just for those with special needs.

iv. It is notable that those who are excluded have very significant levels of learning needs. Some attention needs to be given to these.

v. Teachers who have difficulty in managing pupils are often very isolated and need as much support as possible from their colleagues with systems of caring and opportunities to share problems.

Group C

1. Group C bemoaned the loss of the 'E' in EBD. Concern was expressed that often the support available to teachers assumed that children's learning was more cognitively based without reference to the emotional content. Children who do not do well are often marginalised. League tables are not necessarily wrong in principle, but need to be more sensitively assembled and presented.

2. The quality of teacher support needs to be improved. How do we encourage professionals to work more closely together? EPs are currently less involved in intervention than in statutory assessment procedures. Sometimes the local teachers are more informed in relation to intervention strategies than the psychologists. We must be aware of de-skilling teachers and enable professionals to talk honestly to each other, sharing their problems and their solutions.

Group D

1. Group D discussed a range of issues concerning emotions, psychological development and mental health. These are difficult concepts for education to express in policy terms. Perhaps a policy statement could be that: 'schools should be places in which to develop children's emotional well-being'.

2. A number of concerns were raised with reference to special schools - what does it mean culturally to be sent to a special school? Should we be thinking of all schools as special with EBD schools having specialists in emotional development? There is a significant lack of training for those working with EBD children. Regional planning might be a positive step forward in order to provide a network of provision.

3. The contents of statements is often unhelpful. Do we need to re-visit the way in which statements are drawn up? Do we need to be profiling

students and schools so as to create a better match? What is effective multi-agency working? Often children are involved with a number of professionals from different agencies but in practice they work quite separately and do not communicate with each other.

Group E
1. The barriers across agencies which prevent easy communication are functional. They address problem of matching infinite need with finite resources. How should we measure the success of a system? Whatever we came up with, we would want it to ensure that children remain visible and are not hidden within the system, as well as making sure that there is a link between the local school and any provision that is made for such children. We need to encourage schools to accept responsibility for their pupils.

2. The system can 'lose' children. What would happen if we expected schools to provide ongoing support for pupils after exclusions?

General discussion
1. Not much mention has been made at this seminar of the wishes and feelings of parents and families. Parents of EBD pupils do not group together. There is no pressure group or significant voluntary organisation for such pupils, except perhaps for those with ADD/ADHD where parents are beginning to group together. They are coming together and saying it is respectable to have a child whose behaviour challenges the system.

2. How do we help pupils and parents of pupils with behavioural difficulties to benefit from their rights within the system? Some parent partnership schemes are trying to support parents of EBD pupils. But parents often feel blame and perceptions of their own inadequacy may colour relationships with schools and professionals.

3. We tend to make an unhelpful distinction in our perceptions of schools and parents, regarding schools as responsible for learning and parents as responsible for behaviour - this leads to a culture of putting blame upon parents and schools if problems arise.

4. In considering multi-professional approaches, the stronger the multi-professional approach becomes the more it is possible that the

non-professionals are shut out. It is not good enough for professionals to say: 'this is our professional judgement' without taking into account the views of governors and others involved with the child. Governing bodies are often not well enough informed and do not have sufficient information put in front of them in order to make proper judgements and decisions. It is not easy for governors to change their decisions once they are made. The non-professionals need to be involved with the professionals before decisions are made. Schools, parents and governors need mutual understanding of each other's roles, responsibilities and competencies.

5. One central issue concerns the pressure that teachers feel is put upon them. It is difficult if not impossible for certain types of interaction and understanding to take place. Teachers are asked to contribute to multi-disciplinary teams, to be engaged in community involvement, peer group discussions and support, social support from within the school and working with parents. They need a bit of time in which they can reflect. Following reflection they could then collaborate more and move into a situation of support but they seldom have time and feel exhausted.

6. It is important that schools should feel led by an LEA who can establish a quality framework in which to establish standards. In Essex the LEA is attempting to provide such a framework which sets personal/social development of the child as an important area for staff discussion and staff development. Schools need a 'critical friend' and the LEA can perform this role. They need to discuss practical ways of supporting children. Essex LEA are Kitemarking schools whose basic performance against key objectives within the LEA framework have been achieved. This provides a baseline of practice for handling the majority of children although there would always be some whose problems lie outside the general range.

7. The issue of time is very important; time to promote emotional development. Schools require time for reflection. Even if schools support a facility to provide internal support, few can make use of this provision because there is not enough time allocated. How do you balance the more qualitative elements of child and social development, such as the emotions, against the quantitative approaches adopted by most schools?

8. As time in school is at such a premium, what activity should be promoted in order to make best use of the time available? Priorities need to be set as part of the senior management's responsibilities in the overall management of time. A collective staff view should be obtained in order to inform decisions. A key issue is how to break the spiral of escalating challenging behaviour. Currently the social development of children is insufficiently acknowledged within the context of overall school development.

9. There is a danger that teachers might have a view that it is all 'within child'. But many teachers do in fact see that they have a contributing part to play in the way in which children behave and respond. Many teachers do accept that they may be part of the problem.

10.The general context in which education currently takes place is not conducive to progress in terms of how teachers handle their emotions and deal with pupils' behaviour. There is an ethos of blame. How you present the data on exclusions and pupil behaviour is important. There is no LEA at present that is truly adopting an inclusive approach. 'Inclusive' LEAs who are attempting to adopt such policies throughout their system say 'that we are a long way from being truly an inclusive authority', even though they are committed to the general principles. There is a difference between saying that all pupils will be included in school as opposed to developing an inclusive system where the needs of all pupils are recognised and provided for.

Speakers' responses
Greg Richardson
1. We are sceptical about league tables. Hospitals have league tables and Great Ormond Street casualty department has a five star rating but it has no casualty department! Criteria driven services may forget the holistic needs of children and ignore the extent to which these may influence the child's educational performance.

2. How can a child psychiatrist support school staff or, at least not make their lives worse? Beyond the issue of abuse 'I don't care what you do as long as you do it confidently'. The cycle of blame - leading to guilt - leading to recompense, can make things worse. How do we get this message across to teachers?

3. Anxiety is the emotion that drives everything. Why do teachers get so anxious? They get anxious prior to OFSTED inspections.

The issue of time is important although good agencies make time available. An effective head can make time available for professionals to work together even in very busy situations.

Policies are important because they do provide a good way of relieving anxiety and making more people feel secure.

John Bangs

1. The issue of being confident and possibly being selfish is a live issue. Anxiety and stress are becoming out of control in our environment. The issue of school inspection is contributing to this underlying stress. Teachers are expected to perform 'on the day'. They do not have another chance to demonstrate their effectiveness. This is not a good way of improving the system. The pre-preparation work that they have to do for inspection is also stressful.

2. The role of headteacher as leader is also crucial. I hadn't realised until recently how much anxiety is generated within headteachers and how much time they want to spend sharing their particular difficulties. They feel isolated and lonely.

3. Schools require critical friends from outside. There is a strong perception of teachers that they are working in a context of blame. It is hard for governors to get information about day-to-day working within schools. There is a need to evaluate what governors do since there is a view that governors are above criticism because they are voluntary. Are they, however, effective?

4. Many schools and LEAs are moving towards an inclusive policy but it is difficult to get schools, LEAs and the Government to listen carefully as to what provision can be offered in relation to the needs of pupils.

Tony Dessent (summing up in place of Peter Gray)
I have three pleas:

i. To resist EBD being separated from special educational needs in general. We must maintain the importance of the individual - in terms of assessment, planning, the rights of pupils and parents, and in provision. Those responsible for pupils with special needs must also make allowance for the other pupils.

ii. Keep trying to find ways to collaborate together and to maintain the visibility of each individual pupil (with behaviour difficulties). We must not lose sight of the individual. We must work together within schools and across schools and with the community and other agencies.

iii. We must recognise that this is a hard slog and that there is not an easy or early solution to the problem. We must recognise that the education system is trying to respond to some massive social and educational challenges and that meeting the needs of all these pupils is inevitably going to be problematic. But we must resist the often arbitrary divide between 'SEN' and 'EBD'.

Concluding comments:

The Policy Seminar recorded in this Paper took place a couple of months before the General Elections. Education has become a priority policy area for the new Labour Government, though it is early days to see how policies and practice in the behaviour management and emotional and behavioural difficulties areas will change.

However, the new Education Act 1997 introduced by the last Government and supported by Labour when in opposition will come into operation later this year. This covers matters concerned with behaviour and discipline. In particular, it requires that school Governing Bodies must ensure that policies are pursued which 'promote good behaviour and discipline' and they must publish a writtten statement about principles on discipline. Headteachers are required while acting in accordance with the Governors' statement to decide on appropriate measures and these need to be publicised among parents, pupils and staff. LEAs must also publish a statement about their arrangements for pupils with behavioural difficulties, including support provided to schools to promote good discipline and what provision they make for excluded pupils. Schools can now detain pupils after school without parental consent and pupils can be excluded for up to 45 days a year, not the 15 days a term as before. Exclusion appeals committees are also required when considering whether to reinstate an excluded pupil, to have regard for other pupils and the staff as well as the excluded pupil.

A new White Paper has also been issued with the timetable for an accompanying Green Paper in the field of Special Educational Needs. The proposals in the White Paper aim to tackle problems at an early stage and so prevent difficulties developing into special educational needs. The emphasis is on 'preventive and remedial' action and away from processes leading to statementing. There is a continued commitment to mainstreaming and rights for disabled people, but an acknowledgement that there may be a requirement for specialist and even residential schooling. This is presented as compatible with the principles of inclusive education. There is also reference to some cross-LEA planning to ensure specialist provision. A newly established National Advisory group on SEN chaired by the Minister responsible for SEN will advise on the Green Paper, a consultative document, which will be used with regional meetings to seek wider views on special educational needs policy and practice. The publication of this Policy Paper on emotional and behavioural difficulties is therefore most timely for this consultative process.